DINNER!

WEEKNIGHT MEALS FOR BUSY FAMILIES

Publications International, Ltd.

Pictured on the front cover (*clockwise from top left*): Cavatappi with Sausage Meatballs (*page 125*), Simple Chicken Pasta Toss (*page 79*), and Chicken Pot Pie (*page 102*).

Pictured on the back cover (*clockwise from top left*): Wild Rice Soup (*page 6*), Kale, Mushroom and Caramelized Onion Pizza (*page 32*), Tuna-Macaroni Casserole (*page 104*), and Spicy Beef Tacos (*page 128*).

ISBN: 978-1-4508-9351-0

Library of Congress Control Number: 2014944759

Manufactured in China.

8 7 6 5 4 3 2 1

Microwave Cooking: Microwave ovens vary in wattage. Use the cooking times as guidelines and check for doneness before adding more time.

Publications International, Ltd.

TABLE OF CONTENTS

SOUPS, CHILIES & CHOWDERS

Fresh Tomato Pasta Soup

FRESH TOMATO PASTA SOUP

1 **tablespoon olive oil**

½ **cup chopped onion**

1 **clove garlic, minced**

3 **pounds fresh tomatoes (about 9 medium), coarsely chopped**

3 **cups fat-free reduced-sodium chicken broth**

1 **tablespoon minced fresh basil**

1 **tablespoon minced fresh marjoram**

1 **tablespoon minced fresh oregano**

1 **teaspoon whole fennel seeds**

½ **teaspoon black pepper**

¾ **cup uncooked rosamarina, orzo or other small pasta**

½ **cup (2 ounces) shredded part-skim mozzarella cheese**

1. Heat oil in large saucepan over medium heat. Add onion and garlic; cook and stir until onion is tender.

2. Add tomatoes, broth, basil, marjoram, oregano, fennel seeds and pepper; bring to a boil. Reduce heat to low; cover and simmer 25 minutes. Remove from heat; cool slightly.

3. Purée tomato mixture in batches in food processor or blender. Return to saucepan; bring to a boil. Add pasta; cook 7 to 9 minutes or until tender. Sprinkle with mozzarella cheese.

Makes 8 servings

WILD RICE SOUP

½ **cup dried lentils, rinsed and sorted**

1 **package (6 ounces) long grain and wild rice blend**

1 **can (about 14 ounces) vegetable broth**

1 **bag (10 ounces) frozen mixed vegetables**

1 **cup milk**

2 **slices (1 ounce each) American cheese, cut into pieces**

1. Place lentils in small saucepan; cover with about 3 cups water. Bring to a boil over medium-high heat. Reduce heat to low. Simmer, covered, 5 minutes. Let stand, covered, 1 hour. Drain and rinse lentils.

2. Cook rice according to package directions. Add lentils, broth, mixed vegetables, milk and cheese. Bring to a boil over medium-high heat. Reduce heat to low. Simmer, uncovered, 20 minutes.

Makes 6 servings

SLOW COOKER CHEESE SOUP

2 cans (10¾ ounces each) condensed cream of celery soup, undiluted

4 cups (16 ounces) shredded Cheddar cheese

1 teaspoon paprika, plus additional for garnish

1 teaspoon Worcestershire sauce

1¼ cups half-and-half

Salt and black pepper

Snipped fresh chives (optional)

SLOW COOKER DIRECTIONS

1. Combine soup, cheese, 1 teaspoon paprika and Worcestershire sauce in slow cooker. Cover; cook on LOW 2 to 3 hours.

2. Add half-and-half; stir until blended. Cover; cook on LOW 20 minutes. Season to taste with salt and pepper. Sprinkle with additional paprika and snipped chives.

Makes 4 servings

1 **pound uncooked dried black beans**

Cold water

6 **cups water**

1 **whole bay leaf**

3 **tablespoons vegetable oil**

2 **large onions, chopped**

3 **cloves garlic, minced**

1 **can (about 14 ounces) diced tomatoes**

2 **to 3 fresh or canned jalapeño peppers,* stemmed, seeded and minced**

2 **tablespoons chili powder**

1½ **teaspoons salt**

1 **teaspoon paprika**

1 **teaspoon dried oregano**

1 **teaspoon unsweetened cocoa powder**

½ **teaspoon ground cumin**

¼ **teaspoon ground cinnamon**

1 **tablespoon red wine vinegar**

CONDIMENTS (OPTIONAL)

1 **cup plain yogurt or sour cream**

Picante sauce

½ **cup sliced green onions or chopped fresh cilantro**

Jalapeño peppers can sting and irritate the skin, so wear rubber gloves when handling peppers and do not touch your eyes.

1. Sort beans, discarding any foreign material. Place beans in 8-quart Dutch oven. Add enough cold water to cover beans by 2 inches. Cover; bring to a boil over high heat. Boil 2 minutes. Remove from heat; let soak, covered, 1 hour. Drain. Add the 6 cups water and bay leaf to beans in Dutch oven. Return to heat. Bring to a boil. Reduce heat and simmer, partially covered, 1 to 2 hours or until tender.

2. Meanwhile, heat oil in large skillet over medium heat. Add onions and garlic; cook until onions are tender. Coarsely chop tomatoes; add to skillet. Add jalapeño peppers, chili powder, salt, paprika, oregano, cocoa, cumin and cinnamon. Simmer 15 minutes. Add tomato mixture to beans. Stir in vinegar. Continue simmering 30 minutes or until beans are very tender and chili has thickened slightly. Remove and discard bay leaf. Ladle chili into individual bowls. Serve with condiments.

Makes 6 servings

VEGAN VARIATION: Omit sour cream

SENSATIONAL CHICKEN NOODLE SOUP

4 cups SWANSON® Chicken Broth (Regular, Natural Goodness® *or* Certified Organic)

Generous dash ground black pepper

1 medium carrot, sliced (about ½ cup)

1 stalk celery, sliced (about ½ cup)

½ cup *uncooked* extra-wide egg noodles

1 cup shredded cooked chicken *or* turkey

1. Heat the broth, black pepper, carrot and celery in a 2-quart saucepan over medium-high heat to a boil.

2. Stir the noodles and chicken into the saucepan. Reduce the heat to medium. Cook for 10 minutes or until the noodles are tender.

Makes 4 servings

ASIAN SOUP: Add **2** green onions cut into ½-inch pieces, **1 clove** garlic, minced, **1 teaspoon** ground ginger and **2 teaspoons** soy sauce. Substitute **uncooked** curly Asian noodles for egg noodles.

MEXICAN SOUP: Add **½ cup** PACE® Chunky Salsa, **1 clove** garlic, minced, **1 cup** rinsed and drained black beans and **½ teaspoon** chili powder. Substitute **2** corn tortillas (4- or 6-inch) cut into thin strips for the noodles, adding them just before serving.

ITALIAN TORTELLINI SOUP: Add **1 can** (about 14.5 ounces) diced tomatoes, drained, **1 clove** garlic, minced, **1 teaspoon** dried Italian seasoning, crushed, and **1 cup** spinach leaves. Substitute **½ cup** frozen cheese tortellini for egg noodles. Serve with grated Parmesan cheese.

6 to 8 (6-inch) corn tortillas, preferably day-old

2 large very ripe tomatoes, peeled and seeded (about 1 pound)

⅔ cup coarsely chopped white onion

1 clove garlic

 Vegetable oil

7 cups chicken broth

4 sprigs fresh cilantro

3 sprigs fresh mint (optional)

½ to 1 teaspoon salt

4 or 5 dried pasilla chiles

5 ounces queso Chihuahua or Monterey Jack cheese, cut into ½-inch cubes

¼ cup coarsely chopped fresh cilantro

1. Stack tortillas; cutting through stack, cut tortillas into ½-inch-wide strips. Let strips stand, uncovered, on wire rack 1 to 2 hours to dry slightly.

2. Place tomatoes, onion and garlic in blender; process until smooth. Heat 3 tablespoons oil in saucepan over medium heat until hot. Add tomato mixture. Cook 10 minutes, stirring frequently.

3. Add broth and cilantro sprigs to saucepan; bring to a boil over high heat. Reduce heat to low. Simmer, uncovered, 20 minutes. Add mint, if desired, and salt; simmer 10 minutes more. Remove and discard cilantro and mint. Keep soup warm.

4. Heat ½ inch oil in deep, heavy, large skillet over medium-high heat to 375°F; adjust heat to maintain temperature.

5. Fry half of tortilla strips at a time, in single layer, 1 minute or until crisp, turning strips occasionally. Remove with slotted spoon; drain on paper towels.

6. Fry chiles in same oil about 30 seconds or until puffed and crisp, turning chiles occasionally. *Do not burn chiles.* Drain on paper towels. Cool slightly; crumble coarsely.

7. Ladle soup into bowls. Add chiles, tortilla strips, cheese and chopped cilantro according to taste.

Makes 4 to 6 servings

SIMPLE HAMBURGER SOUP

2 **pounds ground beef or turkey, cooked and drained**
1 **can (28 ounces) whole tomatoes, undrained**
2 **cans (14 ounces each) beef broth**
1 **bag (10 ounces) frozen gumbo soup vegetables**
½ **cup uncooked pearl barley**
1 **teaspoon salt**
1 **teaspoon dried thyme**
  Black pepper

SLOW COOKER DIRECTIONS

Combine all ingredients in slow cooker. Add water to cover. Cover; cook on HIGH 3 to 4 hours or until barley and vegetables are tender.

Makes 8 servings

CLAM CHOWDER

2 cans (6.5 ounces each) clams

1½ cups milk

⅔ cup instant mashed potato flakes

2 tablespoons butter

1 teaspoon minced onion

½ teaspoon dried parsley flakes

¼ teaspoon ground white pepper

¼ teaspoon paprika (optional)

½ cup oyster crackers

MICROWAVE DIRECTIONS

Combine clams, milk, potato flakes, butter, onion, parsley and pepper in medium microwavable dish. Microwave on HIGH 2 minutes. Stir. Microwave on HIGH 2 minutes or until creamy and heated through. Garnish with paprika. Serve with crackers.

Makes 2 servings

Nonstick cooking spray

2 **medium onions, thinly sliced**

½ **cup chopped carrot**

½ **cup chopped celery**

½ **cup peeled and chopped turnip**

1 **small jalapeño pepper,* finely chopped**

2 **cups water**

2 **cans (about 14 ounces each) vegetable broth**

1 **can (about 14 ounces) no-salt-added stewed tomatoes**

8 **ounces dried lentils, sorted, rinsed and drained**

2 **teaspoons chili powder**

½ **teaspoon dried oregano**

3 **ounces uncooked whole wheat spaghetti, broken**

¼ **cup minced fresh cilantro**

*Jalapeño peppers can sting and irritate the skin, so wear rubber gloves when handling peppers and do not touch your eyes.

1. Spray large nonstick saucepan with cooking spray; heat over medium heat. Add onions, carrot, celery, turnip and jalapeño pepper; cook and stir 10 minutes or until vegetables are crisp-tender.

2. Add water, broth, tomatoes, lentils, chili powder and oregano; bring to a boil. Reduce heat; simmer, covered, 20 to 30 minutes or until lentils are tender.

3. Add pasta; cook 10 minutes or until tender. Ladle soup into bowls; sprinkle with cilantro.

Makes 6 servings

4 **bacon slices, diced**

2 **pounds boneless beef top round or chuck shoulder steak, trimmed and cut into ½-inch cubes**

1 **medium onion, chopped**

2 **cloves garlic, minced**

¼ **cup chili powder**

1 **teaspoon dried oregano**

1 **teaspoon ground cumin**

1 **teaspoon salt**

½ **to 1 teaspoon ground red pepper**

½ **teaspoon hot pepper sauce**

4 **cups water**

Additional chopped onion (optional)

1. Cook bacon in 5-quart Dutch oven over medium-high heat until crisp. Remove with slotted spoon; drain on paper towels.

2. Add half of beef to bacon drippings in Dutch oven; cook and stir until lightly browned. Remove beef to plate; repeat with remaining beef.

3. Add onion and garlic to Dutch oven; cook and stir over medium heat until onion is tender. Return beef and bacon to Dutch oven. Stir in chili powder, oregano, cumin, salt, ground red pepper, hot pepper sauce and water; bring to a boil over high heat.

4. Reduce heat to low; cover and simmer 1½ hours. Skim fat from surface; simmer, uncovered, 30 minutes or until beef is very tender and chili has thickened slightly. Garnish with additional chopped onion.

Makes 6 servings

GREEN & YELLOW SPLIT PEA SOUP

1 to 2 smoked ham hocks or meaty ham bones

5 to 6 cups water

¾ cup dried green split peas, rinsed and sorted

¾ cup dried yellow split peas, rinsed and sorted

1 package dry vegetable soup mix

1 teaspoon chicken bouillon granules

1 whole bay leaf

½ teaspoon lemon-pepper seasoning

SLOW COOKER DIRECTIONS

1. Combine ham hocks, water, peas, dry soup mix, bouillon granules, bay leaf and lemon-pepper seasoning in slow cooker. Cover; cook on LOW 4 to 5 hours.

2. Remove and discard bay leaf. Remove ham hock; remove skin. Cut meat from bones; discard bones. Return meat to slow cooker. Cover; cook on LOW 15 minutes or until heated through.

Makes 4 to 5 servings

CONVENTIONAL METHOD: Simmer bean mixture in Dutch oven, partially covered, 1 hour or until peas are tender. Continue as directed in step 2.

POTATO CHEDDAR SOUP

2 **pounds new red potatoes, cut into ½-inch cubes**

3 **cups chicken or vegetable broth**

¾ **cup coarsely chopped carrots**

1 **medium onion, coarsely chopped**

½ **teaspoon salt**

1 **cup half-and-half**

¼ **teaspoon black pepper**

2 **cups (8 ounces) shredded Cheddar cheese**

SLOW COOKER DIRECTIONS

1. Place potatoes, broth, carrots, onion and salt in slow cooker. Cover; cook on LOW 6 to 7 hours or on HIGH 3 to 3½ hours or until vegetables are tender.

2. Stir in half-and-half and pepper. Cover; cook on HIGH 15 minutes. Turn off heat. Let stand, uncovered, 5 minutes. Stir in cheese until melted.

Makes 6 servings

CREAMY CHICKEN AND RICE SOUP

2 **cups water**

2 **cans (3 ounces each) chunk chicken, undrained**

½ **cup uncooked instant rice**

1 **package (2 ounces) white cream sauce mix**

2 **tablespoons chopped onion**

¾ **teaspoon chicken bouillon granules**

¼ **teaspoon ground white pepper**

MICROWAVE DIRECTIONS

Place water, chicken, rice, sauce mix, onion, bouillon granules and pepper in medium microwavable mug or bowl. Microwave on HIGH 6 to 8 minutes or until heated through. Let stand, covered, 5 minutes. Stir before serving.

Makes 1 serving

NEW ENGLAND FISH CHOWDER

¼ **pound bacon, diced**

1 **cup chopped onion**

½ **cup chopped celery**

2 **cups diced russet potatoes**

2 **tablespoons all-purpose flour**

2 **cups water**

1 **teaspoon salt**

1 **whole bay leaf**

1 **teaspoon dried dill**

½ **teaspoon dried thyme**

½ **teaspoon black pepper**

1 **pound cod, haddock or halibut fillets, skinned, boned and cut into 1-inch pieces**

2 **cups milk or half-and-half**

1. Cook bacon in 5-quart Dutch oven over medium-high heat, stirring occasionally. Drain on paper towels.

2. Add onion and celery to drippings; cook and stir until onion is soft. Add potatoes; cook and stir 1 minute. Add flour; cook and stir 1 minute. Add water, salt, bay leaf, dill, thyme and pepper; bring to a boil over high heat. Reduce heat to low. Cover and simmer 25 minutes or until potatoes are fork-tender.

3. Add fish; simmer, covered, 5 minutes or until fish begins to flake when tested with fork. Remove and discard bay leaf. Add bacon to chowder. Add milk; heat through. *Do not boil.*

Makes 4 to 6 servings

PIZZAS & PASTA

Quick Pasta Puttanesca

QUICK PASTA PUTTANESCA

- **1 package (16 ounces) uncooked spaghetti or linguine**
- **3 tablespoons plus 1 teaspoon olive oil, divided**
- **¼ to 1 teaspoon red pepper flakes***
- **1 tablespoon dried minced onion**
- **1 teaspoon minced garlic**
- **2 cans (about 6 ounces each) chunk light tuna packed in water, drained**
- **1 can (28 ounces) diced tomatoes**
- **1 can (8 ounces) tomato sauce**
- **24 pitted kalamata or black olives**
- **2 tablespoons capers, drained**

For a mildly spicy dish, use ¼ teaspoon red pepper flakes. For a very spicy dish, use 1 teaspoon red pepper flakes.

1. Cook spaghetti according to package directions; drain and return to saucepan. Add 1 teaspoon oil; toss to coat. Cover and keep warm.

2. Heat remaining 3 tablespoons oil in large skillet over medium-high heat. Add pepper flakes; cook and stir until sizzling. Add onion and garlic; cook and stir 1 minute. Add tuna; cook and stir 2 to 3 minutes. Add tomatoes, tomato sauce, olives and capers. Cook until sauce is heated through, stirring frequently.

3. Add sauce to pasta; mix well. Serve immediately.

Makes 6 to 8 servings

BOWTIE PASTA WITH GARLIC VEGETABLES

3 medium carrots, thinly sliced

2 small zucchini, thinly sliced

¼ cup (½ stick) butter

1 large onion, chopped

4 cloves garlic, minced

½ cup vegetable broth

½ cup whipping cream

½ teaspoon salt

½ teaspoon dried tarragon

¼ teaspoon black pepper

2 cups hot cooked bowtie pasta

1. Place carrots and zucchini in large saucepan; add water to cover. Cook, uncovered, 3 minutes or until crisp-tender. Drain; set aside.

2. Melt butter in same saucepan. Add onion and garlic; cook until tender. Gradually stir in broth, cream, salt, tarragon and pepper; simmer 5 minutes or until sauce is slightly thickened. Add vegetables; cook until heated through, stirring occasionally. Add pasta to sauce; toss lightly. Serve immediately.

Makes 4 servings

ENGLISH MUFFIN PEPPERONI PIZZAS

INGREDIENTS

- ¾ **cup pizza sauce**
- 6 **English muffins, halved**
- 1½ **cups (6 oz.) SARGENTO® Shredded Mozzarella Cheese**
- 3 **oz. sliced pepperoni**

DIRECTIONS

• Spread pizza sauce on each muffin half. Sprinkle cheese over sauce; top with pepperoni slices.

• Place on baking sheet. Bake in preheated 425°F oven 5 minutes or until cheese is melted.

Makes 6 servings

MEDITERRANEAN MAC & CHEESE

8 ounces uncooked elbow macaroni or other small pasta shape

1 tablespoon olive oil

1 red bell pepper, cut into slivers

1 bunch (about ¾ pound) asparagus, cut into bite-size pieces

4 tablespoons butter, divided

¼ cup all-purpose flour

1¾ cups milk, heated

1 teaspoon minced fresh thyme

Salt and black pepper

1 cup (4 ounces) shredded mozzarella cheese

1 cup bite-size pieces cooked chicken

4 ounces garlic and herb flavored goat cheese

¼ cup dry bread crumbs

1. Preheat oven to 350°F. Cook macaroni according to package directions until almost al dente. Rinse under cold running water to stop cooking; set aside.

2. Meanwhile, heat oil in medium skillet over medium-high heat; cook and stir bell pepper 3 minutes. Add asparagus; cook and stir 3 minutes or until crisp-tender. Remove from skillet.

3. Melt 3 tablespoons butter over medium-low heat in large saucepan or deep skillet until bubbly. Whisk in flour until smooth paste forms; cook and stir 2 minutes without browning. Gradually whisk in milk. Turn heat to medium; cook 6 to 8 minutes, whisking constantly until mixture begins to bubble and thickens slightly. Add thyme and season with salt and black pepper. Remove from heat.

4. Stir in mozzarella cheese until melted. Combine pasta, bell pepper, asparagus and chicken with cheese sauce. Crumble goat cheese into mixture and transfer to 2-quart casserole. Top with bread crumbs and dot with remaining 1 tablespoon butter.

5. Bake 25 to 30 minutes or until lightly browned and bubbly.

Makes 4 to 6 servings

KALE, MUSHROOM AND CARAMELIZED ONION PIZZA

1 **package (13.8 ounces) refrigerated pizza dough**

1 **tablespoon olive oil**

1 **cup chopped yellow onion**

1 **package (8 ounces) sliced mushrooms**

3 **cloves garlic, minced**

4 **cups packed coarsely chopped kale**

¼ **teaspoon red pepper flakes**

½ **cup pizza sauce**

¾ **cup (3 ounces) finely shredded part-skim mozzarella cheese**

1. Preheat oven to 425°F. Spray 15×10-inch jelly-roll pan with nonstick cooking spray. Unroll pizza dough on prepared pan. Press dough evenly into pan and ½ inch up sides. Prick dough all over with fork. Bake 7 to 10 minutes or until lightly browned.

2. Heat oil in large nonstick skillet over medium heat. Add onion; cook and stir 8 minutes or until golden brown. Add mushrooms and garlic; cook and stir 4 minutes. Add kale and pepper flakes; cover and cook 2 minutes to wilt kale. Uncover; cook and stir 3 to 4 minutes or until vegetables are tender.

3. Spread pizza sauce over crust. Spread kale mixture evenly over sauce; top with cheese. Bake 10 minutes or until crust is golden brown.

Makes 4 servings

NOTE: Kale has tough stems that should be removed before cooking. To trim away tough stems, make a "V-shaped" cut where the stem joins the leaf. Stack the leaves and cut them into pieces.

MOM'S BAKED MOSTACCIOLI

- **1** **container (16 ounces) part-skim ricotta cheese**
- **½** **cup cholesterol-free egg substitute**
- **¼** **cup grated Parmesan cheese**
  - **Garlic powder**
  - **Black pepper**
  - **Italian seasoning**
- **1** **package (16 ounces) mostaccioli, cooked and drained**
- **1** **jar (26 ounces) prepared pasta sauce**
- **1½** **cups (6 ounces) shredded mozzarella cheese**

1. Preheat oven to 350°F. Spray 13×9-inch casserole with nonstick cooking spray.

2. Combine ricotta cheese, egg substitute and Parmesan cheese in medium bowl. Season with garlic powder, pepper and Italian seasoning; mix well.

3. Place half of pasta and half the sauce in prepared casserole. Spread ricotta mixture evenly over pasta. Spoon remaining pasta and sauce over ricotta mixture. Top with mozzarella cheese.

4. Bake 30 minutes or until hot and bubbly.

Makes 8 servings

PAN ROASTED VEGETABLE & CHICKEN PIZZA

Vegetable cooking spray

¾ **pound skinless, boneless chicken breasts, cubed**

3 **cups cut-up vegetables***

⅛ **teaspoon garlic powder *or* 1 clove garlic, minced**

1 **can (10¾ ounces) CAMPBELL'S® Condensed Cream of Mushroom Soup (Regular *or* 98% Fat Free)**

1 **prepared pizza crust (12-inch)**

1 **cup shredded Monterey Jack cheese (about 4 ounces)**

*Use a combination of sliced zucchini, red **or** green pepper cut into 2-inch long strips, and thinly sliced onion.*

1. Spray medium skillet with vegetable cooking spray and heat over medium-high heat 1 minute. Add chicken and cook 10 minutes or until browned, stirring often. Set chicken aside.

2. Remove pan from heat. Spray with cooking spray. Reduce heat to medium. Add vegetables and garlic powder. Cook until tender-crisp. Add soup. Return chicken to pan. Heat through.

3. Spread chicken mixture over pizza crust to within ¼ inch of edge. Top with cheese. Bake at 450°F. for 12 minutes or until cheese is melted.

Makes 4 servings

BROCCOLI AND BEEF PASTA

2 cups broccoli florets *or* 1 package (10 ounces) frozen broccoli, thawed

1 onion, thinly sliced

½ teaspoon dried basil

½ teaspoon dried oregano

½ teaspoon dried thyme

1 can (about 14 ounces) Italian-style diced tomatoes

¾ cup beef broth

1 pound lean ground beef

2 cloves garlic, minced

2 cups cooked rotini pasta

¾ cup (3 ounces) grated Parmesan cheese *or* shredded Cheddar cheese

2 tablespoons tomato paste

SLOW COOKER DIRECTIONS

1. Layer broccoli, onion, basil, oregano, thyme, tomatoes and broth in slow cooker. Cover; cook on LOW 2½ hours.

2. Cook and stir beef and garlic in large nonstick skillet over medium-high heat 6 to 8 minutes, stirring to break up meat. Drain fat. Remove beef mixture to slow cooker. Cover; cook on LOW 2 hours.

3. Stir in pasta, cheese and tomato paste. Cover; cook on LOW 30 minutes or until cheese melts and mixture is heated through. Sprinkle with additional cheese, if desired.

Makes 4 servings

SERVING SUGGESTION: Serve with garlic bread.

BBQ CHICKEN SKILLET PIZZA

1 **pound frozen bread dough, thawed**

1 **tablespoon olive oil**

2 **cups shredded cooked chicken***

¾ **cup barbecue sauce, divided**

¼ **cup (1 ounce) shredded mozzarella cheese**

¼ **cup thinly sliced red onion**

½ **cup (2 ounces) shredded smoked Gouda**

Chopped fresh cilantro (optional)

Use a rotisserie chicken for best flavor and convenience.

1. Preheat oven to 425°F. Roll out dough into 15-inch circle on lightly floured surface. Brush oil over bottom and side of large (12-inch) cast iron skillet; place in oven 5 minutes to preheat.

2. Combine chicken and ½ cup barbecue sauce in medium bowl; toss to coat. Remove hot skillet from oven; press dough into bottom and about 1 inch up side of skillet.

3. Spread remaining ¼ cup barbecue sauce over dough. Sprinkle with mozzarella; top with chicken mixture. Sprinkle with half of onion and Gouda cheese; top with remaining onion.

4. Bake about 25 minutes or until crust is golden brown. Garnish with cilantro.

Makes 4 to 6 servings

PASTA PRIMAVERA

⅓ **cup broccoli florets**

⅓ **cup cauliflower florets**

1 **carrot, peeled and thinly sliced**

1 **tablespoon olive oil**

⅓ **cup thinly sliced red bell pepper**

⅓ **cup thinly sliced yellow bell pepper**

⅓ **cup snow peas**

⅛ **cup sliced shiitake, morel or chanterelle mushrooms**

1 **clove garlic, minced**

1 **package (16 ounces) linguine, cooked and drained**

4 **fresh basil leaves, minced *or* 2 teaspoons minced fresh chervil**

1. Steam broccoli, cauliflower and carrot 3 minutes or until crisp-tender.

2. Heat oil in large skillet over medium heat. Add steamed vegetables, bell peppers, snow peas, mushrooms and garlic; cook and stir 3 to 5 minutes. Toss with hot linguine in large bowl. Sprinkle with basil; serve immediately.

Makes 4 servings

PASTA WITH SPINACH AND RICOTTA

8 ounces uncooked tri-colored rotini pasta

Nonstick cooking spray

1 package (10 ounces) frozen chopped spinach, thawed and squeezed dry

2 teaspoons minced garlic

1 cup fat-free or part-skim ricotta cheese

½ cup water

3 tablespoons grated Parmesan cheese, divided

Salt and black pepper

1. Cook pasta according to package directions. Drain well; cover and keep warm.

2. Spray large skillet with nonstick cooking spray; heat over medium-low heat. Add spinach and garlic; cook and stir 5 minutes. Stir in ricotta, water and 1½ tablespoons Parmesan cheese. Season with salt and pepper.

3. Add pasta to skillet; stir until well blended. Sprinkle with remaining 1½ tablespoons Parmesan cheese.

Makes 4 servings

TIP: For a special touch, garnish with fresh basil leaves.

SPICY LASAGNA ROLLERS

1½ pounds Italian sausage, casings removed

1 jar (26 ounces) pasta sauce, divided

1 can (8 ounces) tomato sauce

½ cup chopped roasted red pepper

¾ teaspoon Italian seasoning

½ teaspoon red pepper flakes

1 container (15 ounces) ricotta cheese

1 package (10 ounces) frozen chopped spinach, thawed and squeezed dry

2 cups (8 ounces) shredded Italian cheese blend, divided

1 cup (4 ounces) shredded Cheddar cheese, divided

1 egg, lightly beaten

12 lasagna noodles, cooked and drained

1. Preheat oven to 350°F. Spray 13×9-inch baking pan with nonstick cooking spray.

2. Brown sausage in large skillet over medium heat, stirring to break up meat; drain fat. Stir in ½ cup pasta sauce, tomato sauce, roasted red pepper, seasoning and pepper flakes.

3. Combine ricotta cheese, spinach, 1½ cups Italian cheese blend, ½ cup Cheddar cheese and egg in medium bowl. Spread ¼ cup ricotta mixture over each noodle. Top with ⅓ cup sausage mixture. Tightly roll up each noodle from short end. Place rolls, seam side down, in prepared baking pan. Pour remaining pasta sauce over rolls. Sprinkle with remaining ½ cup Italian cheese blend and ½ cup Cheddar cheese. Cover with foil.

4. Bake 30 minutes. Remove foil; bake 15 minutes or until sauce is bubbly.

Makes 12 servings

NOODLES WITH BABY SHRIMP

- **1 package (3¾ ounces) cellophane noodles**
- **3 green onions**
- **1 tablespoon vegetable oil**
- **1 package (16 ounces) frozen mixed vegetables (such as cauliflower, broccoli and carrots)**
- **1 cup vegetable broth**
- **8 ounces cooked frozen baby shrimp**
- **1 tablespoon soy sauce**
- **2 teaspoons dark sesame oil**
- **¼ teaspoon black pepper**

1. Place noodles in large bowl. Cover with boiling water; let stand 10 to 15 minutes or just until softened. Drain noodles. Cut noodles into 5- or 6-inch pieces; set aside. Cut green onions into 1-inch pieces.

2. Heat wok or large skillet over high heat about 1 minute or until hot. Drizzle vegetable oil into wok; heat 30 seconds. Add green onions; stir-fry 1 minute. Add mixed vegetables; stir-fry 2 minutes. Add broth; bring to a boil. Reduce heat to low; cover and cook 5 minutes or until vegetables are crisp-tender.

3. Add shrimp to wok; cook just until thawed. Stir in noodles, soy sauce, sesame oil and pepper; stir-fry until heated through.

Makes 4 to 6 servings

TIP: Cellophane noodles are also called bean thread noodles or glass noodles. These clear, thin noodles are made from mung bean starch and so are gluten-free. They are sold in packages of 6 to 8 tangled bunches in the Asian section of the supermarket.

CAMPANIA STYLE PIZZA

INGREDIENTS

2	**tsp. olive oil**
1	**cup finely diced fresh fennel bulb (1 small bulb)**
4	**cloves garlic, minced**
1	**(10 oz., 12-inch) pre-baked pizza crust**
½	**cup pizza sauce**
2½	**cups (1 dry pint) cherry tomatoes, halved**
1½	**cups (6 oz.) SARGENTO® Chef Blends™ Shredded Pizzeria Cheese**
⅓	**cup thinly sliced fresh basil leaves**

DIRECTIONS

• Heat oil in large nonstick skillet over medium heat. Add fennel; cook, stirring occasionally, 5 minutes. Add garlic; cook 2 minutes.

• Place pizza crust on baking sheet or pizza pan. Spread pizza sauce over crust; top with fennel mixture, tomatoes and cheese.

• Bake on lower oven rack in preheated 400°F oven 12 to 14 minutes or until cheese and crust are golden brown. Cut into wedges; top with basil.

Makes 6 servings

TIP: Use yellow or red cherry tomatoes for bright color.

MINI VEGGIE PIZZA

INGREDIENTS

- ½ **whole grain bagel**
- ¼ **cup CONTADINA® Original Pizza Sauce**
- 2 **Tbsp. DEL MONTE® Sliced Carrots, drained and diced**
- 2 **Tbsp. DEL MONTE® Whole Kernel Corn, drained**
- ¼ **cup shredded low-fat mozzarella cheese**

DIRECTIONS

1. Toast bagel half in a toaster oven on low heat.

2. Spread pizza sauce on the toasted bagel half.

3. Sprinkle carrots, corn and cheese on top.

4. Toast again in the toaster oven on low heat until cheese melts.

Makes 1 serving

SEAFOOD PASTA

½ **cup olive oil**

1 **pound asparagus, trimmed and cut into 1-inch pieces**

1 **cup chopped green onions**

1 **tablespoon plus 2 teaspoons minced garlic**

1 **package (about 16 ounces) linguine, cooked and drained**

1 **pound medium cooked shrimp, peeled**

1 **package (8 ounces) imitation crabmeat**

1 **package (8 ounces) imitation lobster**

1 **can (8 ounces) pitted black olives, drained**

1. Preheat oven to 350°F. Spray 4-quart casserole with nonstick cooking spray.

2. Heat oil in large skillet over medium heat. Add asparagus, green onions and garlic; cook and stir until tender.

3. Combine asparagus mixture, linguine, shrimp, crabmeat, lobster and olives in prepared casserole. Bake 30 minutes or until heated through.

Makes 6 servings

MANICOTTI

- **1** container (15 ounces) ricotta cheese
- **2** cups (8 ounces) shredded mozzarella cheese
- **½** cup cottage cheese
- **2** eggs, beaten
- **2** tablespoons grated Parmesan cheese
- **½** teaspoon minced garlic
- Salt and black pepper
- **1** package (about 8 ounces) uncooked manicotti shells
- **1** pound ground beef
- **1** jar (about 26 ounces) pasta sauce
- **2** cups water

1. Preheat oven to 375°F.

2. Combine ricotta cheese, mozzarella cheese, cottage cheese, eggs, Parmesan cheese, garlic, salt and pepper in large bowl; mix well. Fill manicotti shells with cheese mixture; place in 13×9-inch baking dish.

3. Brown beef in large skillet over medium-high heat 6 to 8 minutes, stirring to break up meat. Drain fat. Stir in pasta sauce and water. Pour sauce over filled manicotti shells.

4. Bake, covered, 1 hour or until sauce is thickened and shells are tender.

Makes 6 servings

PIZZA TURNOVERS

5 **ounces reduced-fat mild Italian turkey sausage**

½ **cup pizza sauce**

1 **package (10 ounces) refrigerated pizza dough**

⅓ **cup shredded reduced-fat Italian cheese blend**

1. Preheat oven to 425°F. Spray baking sheet with olive oil cooking spray.

2. Brown sausage in medium nonstick skillet over medium heat, stirring to break up meat. Drain fat. Add pizza sauce; cook and stir until heated through.

3. Unroll pizza dough onto prepared baking sheet; pat into 12×8-inch rectangle. Cut into six (4-inch) squares. Divide sausage mixture evenly among squares. Sprinkle with cheese. Lift one corner of each square; fold over filling to opposite corner to form triangle. Press edges with tines of fork to seal.

4. Bake 11 to 13 minutes or until golden brown. Serve immediately or freeze.

Makes 6 servings

TIP: To freeze turnovers, remove to wire rack to cool 30 minutes. Individually wrap in plastic wrap; place in freezer container or resealable freezer bag and freeze. To reheat turnovers, preheat oven to 400°F. Place turnovers in ungreased baking pan. Cover loosely with foil. Bake 18 to 22 minutes or until hot. Or, place one turnover on a paper towel-lined microwavable plate. Microwave on DEFROST (30%) 3 to 3½ minutes or until hot, turning once.

SAUSAGE, PEPPERS & ONION PIZZA

- ½ **pound bulk Italian sausage**
- 1 **medium red bell pepper, cut into strips**
- 1 **pre-baked pizza crust (14 inches)**
- 1 **cup spaghetti or pizza sauce**
- 1½ **cups shredded mozzarella cheese**
- 1⅓ **cups FRENCH'S® French Fried Onions**

1. Preheat oven to 450°F. Cook sausage in nonstick skillet over medium heat until browned, stirring frequently; drain. Add bell pepper and cook until crisp-tender, stirring occasionally.

2. Top pizza crust with sauce, sausage mixture and cheese. Bake 8 to 10 minutes or until cheese melts. Sprinkle with French Fried Onions; bake 2 minutes or until onions are golden.

Makes 8 servings

TIP: You may substitute link sausage; remove meat from casing.

HEARTY BEEF LASAGNA

1 **pound ground beef**

1 **jar (32 ounces) pasta sauce**

2 **cups (16 ounces) cottage cheese**

1 **container (8 ounces) sour cream**

8 **uncooked lasagna noodles**

1½ **cups (6 ounces) shredded mozzarella cheese**

½ **cup grated Parmesan cheese**

1 **cup water**

Fresh basil or thyme (optional)

1. Preheat oven to 350°F.

2. Brown beef in large skillet over medium-high heat 6 to 8 minutes, stirring to break up meat. Drain fat. Reduce heat to low. Add pasta sauce; cook and stir occasionally until heated through. Combine cottage cheese and sour cream in medium bowl; blend well.

3. Spread 1½ cups meat sauce in bottom of 13×9-inch baking pan. Place 4 uncooked noodles over sauce. Top with half of cottage cheese mixture, ¾ cup mozzarella cheese, half of remaining meat sauce and ¼ cup Parmesan cheese. Repeat layers starting with uncooked noodles and topping with remaining ¾ cup mozzarella cheese. Pour water around sides of pan. Cover tightly with foil.

4. Bake 1 hour. Remove foil. Bake, uncovered, 20 minutes or until hot and bubbly. Let stand 15 to 20 minutes before cutting. Garnish with basil.

Makes 8 to 10 servings

SKILLET DISHES

Ham & Swiss Penne Skillet

HAM & SWISS PENNE SKILLET

    6 ounces uncooked penne pasta

    2 slices bread, torn into pieces

    5 tablespoons butter, divided

    3 tablespoons all-purpose flour

2¾ cups whole milk

    1 cup frozen corn, thawed

¾ cup frozen peas, thawed

    6 ounces ham, diced

    1 cup (4 ounces) shredded Swiss cheese

½ cup finely chopped green onions

    Salt and black pepper

1. Cook pasta according to package directions. Drain well; keep warm.

2. Place bread in food processor; pulse to form coarse crumbs. Melt 2 tablespoons butter in large skillet over medium heat. Add bread crumbs; cook and stir 2 minutes or until golden. Transfer to plate; set aside.

3. Melt remaining 3 tablespoons butter in same skillet over medium heat. Add flour; whisk 2 minutes or until smooth. Gradually add milk, whisking constantly to blend. Cook and stir 4 minutes or until slightly thickened. Add pasta, corn, peas, ham, cheese and green onions; stir gently to blend. Season with salt and pepper. Cook 4 minutes or until heated through. Sprinkle with bread crumbs. Serve immediately.

Makes 4 servings

SPANISH BRAISED CHICKEN WITH GREEN OLIVES & RICE

2 **pounds bone-in skinless chicken thighs**

1 **teaspoon paprika**

  Nonstick cooking spray

¾ **cup dry sherry**

2¼ **cups water**

1 **can (about 14 ounces) fat-free reduced-sodium chicken broth**

¾ **cup sliced pimiento-stuffed green olives**

1½ **teaspoons dried sage**

1½ **cups uncooked long grain rice**

1. Sprinkle chicken thighs with paprika. Spray large nonstick skillet with cooking spray; heat over medium-high heat. Cook chicken 6 to 8 minutes or until browned on both sides, turning once.

2. Remove chicken from skillet. Add sherry, stirring to scrape up brown bits from bottom of skillet. Add water, broth, olives and sage; bring to a boil. Reduce heat to low. Return chicken to skillet. Cover and simmer 10 minutes.

3. Add rice to liquid around chicken; gently stir to distribute evenly in skillet. Cover; simmer 20 to 25 minutes or until rice is tender and chicken is cooked through (165°F).

Makes 6 servings

MEDITERRANEAN BEEF SKILLET

2½ **cups (about 8 ounces) uncooked whole wheat rotini pasta**

1 **pound ground beef**

½ **teaspoon dried basil**

½ **teaspoon black pepper**

1 **can (about 14 ounces) diced tomatoes with garlic and onion**

1 **can (8 ounces) tomato sauce**

1 **bag (about 7 ounces) baby spinach, coarsely chopped**

1 **can (about 2 ounces) sliced black olives, drained**

½ **cup crumbled herb-flavored feta cheese**

1. Prepare pasta according to package directions; drain. Cover and keep warm.

2. Brown beef in large skillet over medium-high heat 6 to 8 minutes, stirring to break up meat. Drain fat. Stir in basil and pepper.

3. Reduce heat to medium. Add tomatoes, tomato sauce, spinach and olives; mix well. Cook 10 minutes. Stir in pasta; cook 5 minutes or until heated through. Sprinkle with cheese.

Makes 4 servings

SHRIMP AND VEGGIE SKILLET TOSS

¼ **cup reduced-sodium soy sauce**

2 **tablespoons lime juice**

1 **tablespoon sesame oil**

1 **teaspoon grated fresh ginger**

⅛ **teaspoon red pepper flakes**

32 **medium raw shrimp with tails on (about 8 ounces total), rinsed and patted dry**

2 **medium zucchini, cut in half lengthwise and sliced into 6 pieces each**

6 **green onions, trimmed and halved lengthwise**

12 **grape tomatoes**

1. Whisk soy sauce, lime juice, oil, ginger and red pepper flakes in small bowl; set aside.

2. Spray large nonstick skillet with nonstick cooking spray; heat over medium-high heat. Add shrimp; cook and stir 3 minutes or until shrimp are pink and opaque. Remove from skillet.

3. Spray skillet with cooking spray. Add zucchini; cook and stir 4 to 6 minutes or until just crisp-tender. Add onions and tomatoes; cook 1 to 2 minutes. Add shrimp, cook 1 minute. Transfer to large bowl.

4. Add soy sauce mixture to skillet; bring to a boil. Remove from heat. Stir in shrimp and vegetables; gently toss.

Makes 4 servings

NOTE: Shrimp are very low in calories and fat, and high in protein. They're also a good source of vitamin D and vitamin B12. All seafood are very sensitive to temperature, so return shrimp to refrigerator as soon as possible after purchasing.

CHICKEN FRICASSEE

- **1** **whole chicken (about 3 to 4 pounds), cut up**
- **½** **cup all-purpose flour**
- **1** **teaspoon salt**
- **¼** **teaspoon black pepper**
- **2** **to 3 tablespoons vegetable oil**
- **2** **to 3 tablespoons unsalted butter**
- **1½** **cups chicken broth**
- **¾** **teaspoon dried thyme**
- **1½** **cups baby carrots or 1-inch-wide carrot slices**
- **1** **medium onion, cut into wedges**
- **2** **stalks celery, cut into 1-inch slices**

1. Remove skin from chicken, if desired. Cut large chicken breasts in half crosswise. Place flour, salt and pepper in large resealable food storage bag. Add chicken pieces, two or three at a time; seal bag. Shake to coat chicken. Transfer to plate. Repeat with remaining chicken and flour mixture. Reserve remaining flour mixture.

2. Heat 2 tablespoons each oil and butter in 12-inch skillet over medium heat. Add chicken; cook about 8 minutes per side or until lightly browned, adding remaining 1 tablespoon oil and butter, if necessary. Remove from skillet.

3. Stir 2 tablespoons reserved flour mixture into skillet; cook and stir 1 minute. Gradually stir in broth, whisking until smooth. Stir in thyme. Return chicken to skillet. Add carrots, onion and celery; bring to a boil. Cover and reduce heat. Simmer 35 minutes or until chicken is tender. Remove chicken. Bring liquid to a boil; boil gently about 5 minutes or until sauce is desired thickness. Serve chicken with vegetables and sauce.

Makes 4 to 6 servings

CHICKEN & WILD RICE SKILLET DINNER

1 teaspoon reduced-fat margarine

2 ounces boneless skinless chicken breast, cut into strips (about ½ chicken breast)

1 package (5 ounces) long-grain and wild rice mix with seasoning

½ cup water

3 dried apricots, cut up

1. Melt margarine in small skillet over medium-high heat. Add chicken; cook and stir 3 to 5 minutes or until cooked through.

2. Meanwhile, measure ¼ cup of the rice and 1 tablespoon plus ½ teaspoon of the seasoning mix. Reserve remaining rice and seasoning mix for another use.

3. Add rice, seasoning mix, water and apricots to skillet; mix well. Bring to a boil. Cover and reduce heat to low; simmer 25 minutes or until liquid is absorbed and rice is tender.

Makes 1 serving

SKILLET CHICKEN POT PIE

 1 can (10¾ ounces) fat-free reduced-sodium cream of chicken soup, undiluted

1¼ cups fat-free (skim) milk, divided

 1 package (10 ounces) frozen mixed vegetables

 2 cups diced cooked chicken

 ½ teaspoon black pepper

 1 cup buttermilk biscuit baking mix

 ¼ teaspoon dried summer savory leaves or parsley (optional)

1. Combine soup, 1 cup milk, vegetables, chicken and pepper in medium skillet. Bring to a boil over medium heat.

2. Meanwhile, combine biscuit mix and summer savory, if desired, in small bowl. Stir in remaining 3 to 4 tablespoons milk just until soft batter forms.

3. Drop 6 tablespoonfuls batter over chicken mixture; loosely cover and simmer 12 minutes or until dumplings are cooked through, spooning liquid over dumplings once or twice during cooking.

Makes 6 servings

1 **teaspoon chili powder**

½ **teaspoon salt, divided**

4 **lean boneless pork chops (about 1¼ pounds), well trimmed**

2 **cups diced tomatoes**

1 **cup chopped green, red or yellow bell pepper**

¾ **cup thinly sliced celery**

½ **cup chopped onion**

1 **teaspoon dried thyme**

1 **tablespoon hot pepper sauce**

Nonstick cooking spray

2 **tablespoons finely chopped fresh parsley**

1. Rub chili powder and ¼ teaspoon salt evenly over one side of pork chops.

2. Combine tomatoes, bell pepper, celery, onion, thyme and pepper sauce in medium mixing bowl; stir to blend.

3. Lightly coat 12-inch nonstick skillet with cooking spray. Heat over medium-high heat until hot. Add pork chops, seasoned side down; cook 1 minute. Turn pork; top with tomato mixture.

4. Bring to a boil. Reduce heat and simmer, covered, 25 minutes or until pork is tender and mixture has thickened.

5. Transfer pork to serving plates. Increase heat; bring tomato mixture to a boil and cook 2 minutes or until most of the liquid has evaporated. Remove from heat; stir in parsley and remaining ¼ teaspoon salt and spoon over pork.

Makes 4 servings

½ **pound hot Italian turkey sausage, casing removed**

½ **pound 93% lean ground turkey**

2 **stalks celery, sliced**

⅓ **cup chopped onion**

2 **cups marinara sauce**

1⅓ **cups water**

4 **ounces uncooked bowtie pasta**

1 **medium zucchini, halved lengthwise and cut into ½-inch-thick slices (2 cups)**

¾ **cup chopped green or yellow bell pepper**

½ **cup reduced-fat ricotta cheese**

2 **tablespoons finely shredded Parmesan cheese**

½ **cup (2 ounces) shredded part-skim mozzarella cheese**

1. Cook and stir sausage, turkey, celery and onion in large skillet over medium-high heat until turkey is no longer pink. Stir in marinara sauce and water. Bring to a boil. Add pasta; stir. Reduce heat to medium-low; cover and simmer 12 minutes.

2. Stir in zucchini and bell pepper; cover and simmer 2 minutes. Uncover and simmer 4 to 6 minutes or until vegetables are crisp-tender.

3. Meanwhile, combine ricotta and Parmesan in small bowl. Drop by rounded teaspoonfuls on top of mixture in skillet. Sprinkle with mozzarella. Remove from heat; cover and let stand 10 minutes.

Makes 6 servings

DOUBLE TROUBLE TACOS

1 **pound ground beef**

1 **ORTEGA® Grande Taco Dinner Kit—includes 12 hard taco shells, 8 flour soft tortillas, 2 packets (3 ounces) taco sauce and 1 packet (2 ounces) taco seasoning mix**

1 **pound cooked chicken breast, shredded**

1 **can (16 ounces) ORTEGA® Refried Beans**

1 **tomato, diced**

2 **cups shredded lettuce**

1 **cup (4 ounces) shredded Cheddar cheese**

Brown ground beef in large skillet over medium heat 6 to 8 minutes, stirring to break up meat. Drain fat. Add taco seasoning mix from Grande Taco Dinner Kit and ¾ cup water. Mix and set aside.

Heat chicken in second skillet, adding pouch of taco sauce from Dinner Kit.

Spread beans onto flour tortilla. Place yellow corn taco shell inside the flour tortilla. Add ground beef and shredded chicken mixture topped with diced tomatoes, lettuce and cheese.

Makes 8 tacos

TIP: Feel free to replace the ground beef with ground chicken for a Double Trouble Chicken Taco.

SWEET SOUTHERN BARBECUE CHICKEN

- **2 to 3 tablespoons oil, divided**
- **½ cup chopped onion**
- **1 clove garlic, minced**
- **½ cup packed brown sugar**
- **1 teaspoon dry mustard**
- **1 tablespoon honey mustard**
- **1 tablespoon Dijon mustard**
- **1 cup *Coca-Cola*®**
- **2 tablespoons balsamic vinegar**
- **2 tablespoons cider vinegar**
- **2 tablespoons Worcestershire sauce**
- **½ cup ketchup**
- **2 to 3 pounds boneless skinless chicken thighs**

Heat 1 tablespoon oil in medium skillet over medium heat. Add onion and garlic and cook 2 minutes.

Add next 4 ingredients; bring to a boil over medium-high heat, reduce heat and simmer, uncovered, 20 minutes or until sauce thickens.

Add *Coca-Cola*, balsamic vinegar, cider vinegar, Worcestershire sauce and ketchup; stir.

Simmer 15 to 20 minutes, until sauce thickens. Remove from heat.

Heat remaining oil in large skillet over medium-high heat. Add half of chicken and cook until cooked through, about 5 to 7 minutes per side. After turning, brush chicken with barbecue sauce. Brush both sides again with sauce in the last 1 to 2 minutes of cooking. Serve chicken with additional sauce. Repeat with remaining chicken.

Makes 4 servings

WILD RICE, MUSHROOM AND SPINACH SKILLET

⅓ **cup uncooked wild rice**

⅓ **cup uncooked brown rice**

⅓ **cup uncooked long grain white rice**

1½ **cups water**

1 **can (10 ounces) condensed reduced-sodium chicken broth, undiluted**

2 **tablespoons margarine**

2 **cups sliced shiitake mushrooms**

2 **cups quartered cremini (brown) mushrooms**

2 **cups sliced bok choy**

2 **cups shredded spinach leaves**

¼ **cup (1 ounce) crumbled feta cheese**

1. Combine wild rice, brown rice, white rice, water and broth in large saucepan. Bring to a boil over high heat. Reduce heat to low; cover and simmer 45 minutes or until rice is tender.

2. Melt margarine in large skillet over medium heat. Add mushrooms; cook and stir 3 minutes. Add bok choy and spinach; cook and stir 3 minutes or until greens are wilted.

3. Add rice to greens in skillet; stir until blended. Sprinkle with cheese just before serving.

Makes 10 servings

CHICKEN-ORZO SKILLET

1 tablespoon olive oil

1 teaspoon Greek seasoning *or* 1 teaspoon oregano plus dash garlic powder

½ teaspoon grated lemon peel

½ teaspoon black pepper

4 boneless skinless chicken breasts, cut into 1-inch cubes

1 can (about 14 ounces) chicken broth

1¼ cups uncooked orzo pasta

6 ounces pitted green olives, drained

4 cloves garlic, minced

2 cups packed fresh spinach

½ cup crumbled feta cheese, plus additional for garnish

1. Heat oil in large nonstick skillet over medium heat. Add seasoning, lemon peel and pepper; cook and stir just until fragrant. Add chicken; cook and stir 4 minutes.

2. Stir in broth, orzo, olives and garlic. Bring to a boil over high heat. Reduce heat; simmer, partially covered, 15 minutes or until pasta is tender and chicken is cooked through, stirring occasionally.

3. Stir in spinach and feta. Cover; let stand 2 to 3 minutes or until spinach wilts. Garnish with additional feta.

Makes 4 servings

EASY ASIAN CHICKEN SKILLET

2   **packages (3 ounces each) chicken-flavored ramen noodles**
1   **package (10 ounces) frozen broccoli florets, thawed**
1   **package (9 ounces) frozen baby carrots, thawed**
1   **tablespoon vegetable oil**
1   **pound boneless skinless chicken breasts, cut into thin strips**
1   **can (8 ounces) sliced water chestnuts, drained**
¼   **cup stir-fry sauce**

1. Remove seasoning packets from noodles. Save 1 packet for another use.

2. Bring 4 cups water to a boil in large saucepan. Add noodles, broccoli and carrots. Cook over medium-high heat 5 minutes, stirring occasionally; drain.

3. Heat oil in large nonstick skillet over medium-high heat. Add chicken; cook and stir about 8 minutes or until browned.

4. Stir in noodle mixture, water chestnuts, stir-fry sauce and 1 seasoning packet; cook until heated through.

Makes 4 to 6 servings

SIMPLE CHICKEN PASTA TOSS

- **8 ounces uncooked fettuccine or linguine pasta**
- **2 tablespoons vegetable oil**
- **1½ cups broccoli florets and sliced stems**
- **1 cup snow peas**
- **1 cup diagonally sliced carrots**
- **1 package (about 10 ounces) refrigerated fully cooked grilled chicken strips**
- **1 can (about 2 ounces) sliced black olives, drained**
- **¼ cup vinaigrette salad dressing**

1. Cook pasta according to package directions; drain and keep warm.

2. Meanwhile, heat oil in large skillet over medium-high heat. Add broccoli, snow peas and carrots; cook and stir until crisp-tender. Add chicken; heat through.

3. Combine pasta, vegetable mixture and olives in large bowl. Add salad dressing; toss well.

Makes 4 servings

SHRIMP CAPRESE PASTA

- **1 cup uncooked whole wheat penne pasta**
- **2 teaspoons olive oil**
- **2 cups coarsely chopped grape tomatoes**
- **4 tablespoons chopped fresh basil, divided**
- **1 tablespoon balsamic vinegar**
- **2 cloves garlic, minced**
- **¼ teaspoon salt**
- **⅛ teaspoon red pepper flakes**
- **8 ounces medium raw shrimp (with tails on), peeled and deveined**
- **1 cup grape tomatoes, halved**
- **2 ounces fresh mozzarella pearls**

1. Cook pasta according to package directions, omitting salt. Drain, reserving ½ cup cooking water. Set aside.

2. Heat oil in large skillet over medium heat. Add 2 cups chopped tomatoes, reserved ½ cup pasta water, 2 tablespoons basil, vinegar, garlic, salt and red pepper flakes. Cook and stir 10 minutes or until tomatoes begin to soften.

3. Add shrimp and 1 cup halved tomatoes to skillet; cook and stir 5 minutes or until shrimp turn pink and opaque. Add pasta; cook until heated through.

4. Divide mixture evenly among 4 bowls. Top evenly with cheese and remaining 2 tablespoons basil.

Makes 4 servings

SKILLET FISH WITH LEMON TARRAGON "BUTTER"

- **2** **teaspoons reduced-fat margarine**
- **4** **teaspoons lemon juice, divided**
- **½** **teaspoon grated lemon peel**
- **¼** **teaspoon prepared mustard**
- **¼** **teaspoon dried tarragon**
- **⅛** **teaspoon salt**
- **Nonstick cooking spray**
- **2** **lean white fish fillets (4 ounces each),* rinsed and patted dry**
- **¼** **teaspoon paprika**

Cod, orange roughy, flounder, haddock, halibut and sole can be used.

1. Combine margarine, 2 teaspoons lemon juice, lemon peel, mustard, tarragon and salt in small bowl. Blend well with fork; set aside.

2. Coat 12-inch nonstick skillet with cooking spray. Heat over medium heat until hot.

3. Drizzle fillets with remaining 2 teaspoons lemon juice. Sprinkle one side of each fillet with paprika. Place fillets in skillet, paprika side down; cook 3 minutes. Gently turn and cook 3 minutes longer or until opaque in center and flakes easily when tested with fork. Place fillets on serving plates; top with margarine mixture.

Makes 2 servings

PORK AND SWEET POTATO SKILLET

¾ **pound pork tenderloin, cut into 1-inch cubes**

1 **tablespoon plus 1 teaspoon butter, divided**

¼ **teaspoon salt**

⅛ **teaspoon black pepper**

2 **medium sweet potatoes, peeled and cut into ½-inch pieces (about 2 cups)**

1 **small onion, sliced**

¼ **pound reduced-fat smoked turkey sausage, halved lengthwise and cut into ½-inch pieces**

1 **small green or red apple, cored and cut into ½-inch pieces**

½ **cup prepared sweet-and-sour sauce**

2 **tablespoons chopped fresh parsley (optional)**

1. Place pork and 1 teaspoon butter in large nonstick skillet; cook and stir 2 to 3 minutes over medium-high heat or until pork is no longer pink. Season with salt and pepper. Remove from skillet.

2. Add remaining 1 tablespoon butter, potatoes and onion to skillet. Cover; cook and stir over medium-low heat 8 to 10 minutes or until tender.

3. Add pork, sausage, apple and sweet-and-sour sauce to skillet; cook and stir until heated through. Garnish with parsley.

Makes 4 servings

CASSEROLE MEALS

Tuna Penne Casserole

TUNA PENNE CASSEROLE

6 ounces penne pasta, uncooked

1 can (10¾ ounces) condensed cream of chicken soup, undiluted

1 can (about 6 ounces) tuna, drained and flaked

1 cup (4 ounces) shredded sharp Cheddar cheese

½ cup sliced celery

½ cup milk

¼ cup mayonnaise

1 can (4 ounces) sliced water chestnuts, drained

1 jar (2 ounces) chopped pimientos, drained

½ teaspoon salt

Dash black pepper

Pinch celery seeds

1. Preheat oven to 350°F. Spray 2-quart casserole with nonstick cooking spray.

2. Cook pasta according to package directions; drain. Return to saucepan. Add remaining ingredients; mix well. Transfer to prepared casserole.

3. Bake 25 minutes or until hot and bubbly.

Makes 6 servings

CHICKEN BROCCOLI RICE CASSEROLE

- **3 cups cooked long grain rice**
- **4 boneless skinless chicken breasts (about 1 pound), cooked and cut into bite-size pieces**
- **1½ pounds broccoli, cut into bite-size pieces and steamed until tender**
- **2 cans (10¾ ounces each) condensed cream of celery soup, undiluted**
- **¾ cup mayonnaise**
- **½ cup whole milk**
- **2 teaspoons curry powder**
- **3 cups (12 ounces) shredded sharp Cheddar cheese**

1. Preheat oven to 350°F. Grease 13×9-inch baking dish.

2. Spread cooked rice evenly into prepared dish. Top with chicken and broccoli. Mix soup, mayonnaise, milk and curry powder in medium bowl; pour over chicken and broccoli. Top with cheese.

3. Cover loosely with foil. Bake 45 minutes or until cheese melts and casserole is heated through.

Makes 4 to 6 servings

SEAFOOD NEWBURG CASSEROLE

1 can (10¾ ounces) condensed cream of shrimp soup, undiluted

½ cup half-and-half

1 tablespoon dry sherry

¼ teaspoon ground red pepper

2 cans (6 ounces each) lump crabmeat, drained

3 cups cooked rice

¼ pound medium raw shrimp, peeled

¼ pound bay scallops, rinsed and patted dry

1 jar (4 ounces) pimientos, drained and chopped

¼ cup finely chopped fresh parsley

1. Preheat oven to 350°F. Spray 2½-quart casserole with nonstick cooking spray.

2. Whisk soup, half-and-half, sherry and red pepper in large bowl until blended. Pick out and discard any shell or cartilage from crabmeat. Add crabmeat, rice, shrimp, scallops and pimientos to soup mixture; mix well. Transfer mixture to prepared casserole.

3. Bake, covered, 25 minutes or until shrimp and scallops are opaque. Sprinkle with parsley.

Makes 6 servings

CHICKEN VEGGIE CASSEROLE

1 can (10¾ ounces) condensed cheese soup, undiluted

1 cup milk

1½ cups chopped cooked chicken

1 can (about 16 ounces) sliced potatoes

1 can (about 15 ounces) mixed vegetables

2 cups biscuit baking mix

2 tablespoons mayonnaise

1 egg

1. Preheat oven to 400°F.

2. Bring soup and milk to a boil over medium-high heat in large saucepan, stirring constantly. Stir in chicken, potatoes and vegetables. Pour into 13×9-inch baking dish.

3. Combine baking mix, mayonnaise and egg in medium bowl; mix just until crumbly. Sprinkle over chicken mixture.

4. Bake 30 minutes or until browned and bubbly.

Makes 4 to 6 servings

SALMON & NOODLE CASSEROLE

6 ounces uncooked wide egg noodles

1 teaspoon vegetable oil

1 onion, finely chopped

¾ cup thinly sliced carrot

¾ cup thinly sliced celery

1 can (about 15 ounces) salmon, drained, skin and bones discarded

1 can (10¾ ounces) condensed cream of celery soup, undiluted

1 cup (4 ounces) shredded Cheddar cheese

¾ cup frozen peas

½ cup sour cream

¼ cup milk

2 teaspoons dried dill weed

Black pepper

Fresh dill (optional)

1. Preheat oven to 350°F.

2. Cook noodles according to package directions; drain and return to saucepan.

3. Heat oil in large skillet over medium heat. Add onion, carrot and celery; cook and stir 5 minutes or until carrot is crisp-tender. Add salmon, onion mixture, soup, cheese, peas, sour cream, milk, dill weed and pepper to noodles; stir gently until blended. Pour into 2-quart baking dish.

4. Bake, covered, 25 minutes or until hot and bubbly. Garnish with fresh dill.

Makes 4 servings

PIZZA CASSEROLE

  2 **cups uncooked rotini or other spiral pasta**
1½ **pounds ground beef**
  1 **medium onion, chopped**
    Salt and black pepper
  1 **can (about 15 ounces) pizza sauce**
  1 **can (8 ounces) tomato sauce**
  1 **can (6 ounces) tomato paste**
 ½ **teaspoon sugar**
 ½ **teaspoon garlic salt**
 ½ **teaspoon dried oregano**
  2 **cups (8 ounces) shredded mozzarella cheese**
12 **to 15 slices pepperoni**

1. Preheat oven to 350°F. Cook pasta according to package directions; drain.

2. Meanwhile, brown beef with onion in large skillet over medium-high heat 6 to 8 minutes, stirring to break up meat; drain fat. Season with salt and pepper.

3. Combine pasta, pizza sauce, tomato sauce, tomato paste, sugar, garlic salt and oregano in large bowl. Add beef mixture; stir until blended.

4. Place half of mixture in ovenproof skillet or 3-quart casserole; top with 1 cup cheese. Repeat layers. Arrange pepperoni slices on top.

5. Bake 25 to 30 minutes or until heated through and cheese is melted.

Makes 6 servings

CHICKEN ZUCCHINI CASSEROLE

1 package (about 6 ounces) herb-flavored stuffing mix

½ cup (1 stick) butter, melted

2 cups cubed zucchini, blanched and drained

1 can (14 ounces) condensed cream of celery soup, undiluted

1½ cups chopped cooked chicken

1 cup grated carrots

½ cup sour cream

1 onion, chopped

½ cup (2 ounces) shredded Cheddar cheese

1. Preheat oven to 350°F. Combine stuffing mix and butter in medium bowl; reserve 1 cup stuffing. Place remaining stuffing in 13×9-inch baking dish.

2. Combine zucchini, soup, chicken, carrots, sour cream and onion in large bowl. Pour mixture over stuffing in baking dish. Top with remaining 1 cup stuffing and cheese.

3. Bake 40 to 45 minutes or until heated through and cheese is melted.

Makes 8 servings

SILLY SPAGHETTI CASSEROLE

- **8 ounces uncooked spaghetti, broken in half**
- **¼ cup finely grated Parmesan cheese**
- **¼ cup cholesterol-free egg substitute *or* 1 egg**
- **¾ pound ground turkey or ground beef**
- **⅓ cup chopped onion**
- **2 cups pasta sauce**
- **½ (10-ounce) package frozen cut spinach, thawed and squeezed dry**
- **¾ cup (3 ounces) shredded part-skim mozzarella cheese**
- **1 medium red and/or yellow bell pepper**

1. Preheat oven to 350°F. Spray 8-inch square baking dish with nonstick cooking spray.

2. Cook spaghetti according to package directions; drain. Return spaghetti to saucepan. Add Parmesan cheese and egg substitute; toss. Place in prepared baking dish.

3. Spray large nonstick skillet with nonstick cooking spray. Cook turkey and onion in skillet over medium-high heat until meat is lightly browned, stirring to break up meat. Drain fat. Stir in pasta sauce and spinach. Spoon meat mixture over spaghetti in baking dish; sprinkle with mozzarella cheese.

4. Use small cookie cutter to cut decorative shapes from bell pepper; arrange on top of cheese. Cover with foil. Bake 40 to 45 minutes or until bubbling. Let stand 10 minutes. Cut into squares.

Makes 6 servings

CHICKEN POT PIE

1½ **pounds bone-in chicken pieces, skinned**

1 **cup chicken broth**

½ **teaspoon salt**

¼ **teaspoon black pepper**

1 **to 1½ cups reduced-fat (2%) milk**

3 **tablespoons butter**

1 **medium onion, chopped**

1 **cup sliced celery**

⅓ **cup all-purpose flour**

2 **cups frozen mixed vegetables (peas, corn, carrots and green beans), thawed**

1 **tablespoon chopped fresh Italian parsley *or* 1 teaspoon dried parsley flakes (optional)**

½ **teaspoon dried thyme (optional)**

1 **(9-inch) refrigerated pie crust**

1 **egg, lightly beaten**

1. Combine chicken, broth, salt and pepper in large saucepan over medium-high heat; bring to a boil. Reduce heat to low. Cover; simmer 30 minutes or until chicken is cooked through (165°F).

2. Remove chicken and let cool. Pour remaining chicken broth mixture into glass measure. Let stand; spoon off fat. Add enough milk to broth mixture to equal 2½ cups. Remove chicken from bones and cut into ½-inch cubes.

3. Preheat oven to 400°F. Melt butter in same saucepan over medium heat. Add onion and celery; cook and stir 3 minutes or until tender. Stir in flour until well blended. Gradually stir in broth mixture. Cook, stirring constantly, until sauce thickens and boils. Add chicken, vegetables, parsley and thyme, if desired. Pour into 1½-quart casserole.

4. Roll out pie crust to 1 inch larger than diameter of casserole on lightly floured surface. Cut slits in crust to vent; place on top of casserole. Roll edges and cut away extra dough; flute edges. If desired, reroll scraps to cut into decorative designs; place on crust. Brush with beaten egg. Bake 30 minutes until crust is golden brown and filling is bubbly.

Makes about 6 cups or 4 servings

NOTE: You can substitute 2 cups diced cooked chicken for the chicken pieces. Increase chicken broth to 1 (14-ounce) can. Decrease salt to ¼ teaspoon. Combine broth, salt and pepper in glass measure. Add enough milk to equal 2½ cups. Proceed as directed in step 3.

TUNA-MACARONI CASSEROLE

1 cup mayonnaise

1 cup (4 ounces) shredded Swiss cheese

½ cup milk

¼ cup chopped onion

¼ cup chopped red bell pepper

⅛ teaspoon black pepper

2 cans (about 6 ounces each) tuna, drained and flaked

1 package (about 10 ounces) frozen peas

2 cups shell pasta or elbow macaroni, cooked and drained

½ cup dry bread crumbs

2 tablespoons melted butter

Chopped fresh parsley (optional)

1. Preheat oven to 350°F.

2. Combine mayonnaise, cheese, milk, onion, bell pepper and black pepper in large bowl. Add tuna, peas and pasta, toss to coat well. Spoon into 2-quart casserole.

3. Mix bread crumbs with butter in small bowl and sprinkle over top of casserole. Bake 30 to 40 minutes or until heated through. Top with chopped parsley.

Makes 6 servings

MEATLESS MAINSTAYS

Vegetarian Chili

VEGETARIAN CHILI

- 1 **tablespoon vegetable oil**
- 1 **cup finely chopped onion**
- 1 **cup chopped red bell pepper**
- 2 **tablespoons minced jalapeño pepper***
- 1 **clove garlic, minced**
- 1 **can (28 ounces) crushed tomatoes**
- 1 **can (about 15 ounces) black beans, rinsed and drained**
- 1 **can (about 15 ounces) chickpeas, rinsed and drained**
- ½ **cup whole kernel corn**
- ¼ **cup tomato paste**
- 1 **teaspoon sugar**
- 1 **teaspoon ground cumin**
- 1 **teaspoon dried basil**
- 1 **teaspoon chili powder**
- ¼ **teaspoon black pepper**
- **Sour cream and shredded Cheddar cheese (optional)**

Jalapeño peppers can sting and irritate the skin, so wear rubber gloves when handling peppers and do not touch your eyes.

SLOW COOKER DIRECTIONS

1. Heat oil in large nonstick skillet over medium-high heat until hot. Add onion, bell pepper, jalapeño pepper and garlic; cook and stir 5 minutes or until tender.

2. Transfer onion mixture to slow cooker. Add remaining ingredients except sour cream and cheese; mix well. Cover; cook on LOW 4 to 5 hours.

3. Garnish with sour cream and cheese, if desired.

Makes 4 servings

EGGPLANT PARMIGIANA

- **2 eggs, beaten**
- **¼ cup milk**
- **Dash garlic powder**
- **Dash onion powder**
- **Dash salt**
- **Dash black pepper**
- **½ cup seasoned dry bread crumbs**
- **1 large eggplant (about 1½ pounds), cut into ½-inch-thick slices**
- **Vegetable oil**
- **1 jar (about 26 ounces) pasta sauce**
- **4 cups (16 ounces) shredded mozzarella cheese**
- **2½ cups (10 ounces) shredded Swiss cheese**
- **¼ cup grated Parmesan cheese**
- **¼ cup grated Romano cheese**

1. Preheat oven to 350°F. Combine eggs, milk, garlic powder, onion powder, salt and pepper in shallow dish. Place bread crumbs in another shallow dish. Dip eggplant into egg mixture; coat with bread crumbs.

2. Heat ¼ inch oil in large skillet over medium-high heat. Brown eggplant on both sides in batches; drain on paper towels.

3. Spread 3 tablespoons pasta sauce in bottom of 13×9-inch baking dish. Layer half of eggplant, half of mozzarella cheese, half of Swiss cheese and half of remaining sauce in dish. Repeat layers. Sprinkle with Parmesan and Romano cheeses.

4. Bake 30 minutes or until heated through and cheeses are melted.

Makes 4 servings

STIR-FRIED TOFU AND VEGETABLES

1 **cup vegetable oil**

½ **pound firm tofu, drained and cut into ¼-inch-thick slices**

1 **medium yellow onion, cut into wedges**

1 **medium zucchini (½ pound), cut crosswise into chunks**

1 **medium yellow squash (7 ounces), cut into chunks**

8 **mushrooms, cut into thick slices**

1 **small red bell pepper, cut into strips**

4 **ounces fresh snow peas, trimmed**

¼ **cup water**

1 **tablespoon soy sauce**

1 **tablespoon tomato paste**

¼ **teaspoon salt**

⅛ **teaspoon black pepper**

1. Heat oil in wok over medium-high heat about 4 minutes or until hot. Add tofu and fry about 3 minutes per side or until golden brown, turning once. Remove tofu with slotted spatula to baking sheet lined with paper towels; drain. Drain oil from wok, reserving 2 tablespoons.

2. Return reserved oil to wok. Heat over medium heat 30 seconds or until hot. Add onion and stir-fry 1 minute. Add zucchini, yellow squash and mushrooms; stir-fry 7 to 8 minutes or until zucchini and yellow squash are crisp-tender.

3. Add bell pepper, snow peas and water. Stir-fry 2 to 3 minutes or until crisp-tender. Stir in soy sauce, tomato paste, salt and black pepper until well mixed. Add tofu; stir-fry until heated through and coated with sauce. Transfer to serving platter. Serve immediately.

Makes 4 servings

PESTO LASAGNA

1 package (16 ounces) uncooked lasagna noodles

3 tablespoons olive oil

1½ cups chopped onions

3 cloves garlic, finely chopped

3 packages (10 ounces each) frozen chopped spinach, thawed and squeezed dry

Salt and black pepper

3 cups (24 ounces) ricotta cheese

1½ cups pesto sauce

¾ cup grated Parmesan cheese

½ cup pine nuts, toasted*

4 cups (16 ounces) shredded mozzarella cheese

Roasted red pepper strips (optional)

*To toast pine nuts, spread in single layer in heavy skillet. Cook and stir over medium heat 1 to 2 minutes, stirring frequently, until nuts are lightly browned. Immediately remove from skillet.

1. Preheat oven to 350°F. Spray 13×9-inch casserole or lasagna pan with nonstick cooking spray. Partially cook lasagna noodles according to package directions.

2. Heat oil in large skillet over medium-high heat. Cook and stir onions and garlic until translucent. Add spinach; cook and stir about 5 minutes. Season with salt and pepper. Transfer to large bowl.

3. Add ricotta cheese, pesto, Parmesan cheese and pine nuts to spinach mixture; mix well.

4. Layer 5 lasagna noodles, slightly overlapping, in prepared casserole. Top with one third of ricotta mixture and one third of mozzarella. Repeat layers twice.

5. Bake about 35 minutes or until hot and bubbly. Garnish with red bell pepper strips.

Makes 8 servings

MEATLESS MAINSTAYS

BLACK BEAN & RICE STUFFED POBLANO PEPPERS

2 **large or 4 small poblano peppers**

½ **(15-ounce) can black beans, rinsed and drained**

½ **cup cooked brown rice**

⅓ **cup mild or medium chunky salsa**

⅓ **cup shredded reduced-fat Cheddar cheese or pepper Jack cheese, divided**

1. Preheat oven to 375°F. Lightly spray shallow baking pan with nonstick olive oil cooking spray.

2. Cut thin slice from one side of each pepper. Chop pepper slices; set aside. In medium saucepan, cook remaining peppers in boiling water 6 minutes. Drain and rinse with cold water. Remove and discard seeds and membranes.

3. Stir together beans, rice, salsa, chopped pepper and ¼ cup cheese. Spoon into peppers, mounding mixture. Place peppers in prepared pan. Cover with foil. Bake 12 to 15 minutes or until heated through.

4. Sprinkle with remaining cheese. Bake 2 minutes more or until cheese melts.

Makes 2 servings

VEGGIE TOSTADAS

- **1 tablespoon olive oil**
- **1 cup chopped onion**
- **1 cup chopped celery**
- **2 cloves garlic, chopped**
- **1 can (about 15 ounces) red kidney beans, rinsed and drained**
- **1 can (about 15 ounces) Great Northern beans, rinsed and drained**
- **1 can (about 14 ounces) salsa-style diced tomatoes**
- **2 teaspoons mild chili powder**
- **1 teaspoon ground cumin**
- **6 (6-inch) corn tortillas**

  Toppings: chopped fresh cilantro, shredded lettuce, chopped seeded fresh tomatoes, shredded reduced-fat Cheddar cheese and fat-free sour cream (optional)

1. Heat oil in large skillet over medium heat. Add onion, celery and garlic. Cook and stir 8 minutes or until softened. Add beans and diced tomatoes. Stir to blend. Add chili powder and cumin; stir. Reduce heat to medium-low. Simmer 30 minutes, stirring occasionally, until thickened.

2. Meanwhile, preheat oven to 400°F. Place tortillas in single layer directly on oven rack. Bake 10 to 12 minutes or until crisp. Place 1 tortilla on each plate. Spoon bean mixture evenly over each tortilla. Top with cilantro, lettuce, chopped tomatoes, Cheddar cheese and sour cream, if desired.

Makes 6 servings

TOFU STUFFED SHELLS

- 1 can (15 ounces) no-salt-added tomato purée
- 8 ounces mushrooms, thinly sliced
- ½ cup shredded carrot
- ¼ cup water
- 2 cloves garlic, minced
- 1 tablespoon sugar
- 1 tablespoon Italian seasoning
- 12 jumbo uncooked pasta shells
- 1 package (14 ounces) firm tofu, drained and pressed
- ½ cup chopped green onions
- 2 tablespoons grated Parmesan cheese
- 2 tablespoons minced fresh parsley
- 1 tablespoon dried basil
- ½ teaspoon salt
- ¼ teaspoon black pepper
- ½ cup (2 ounces) shredded part-skim mozzarella cheese

1. For sauce, combine tomato purée, mushrooms, carrots, water, garlic, sugar and Italian seasoning in medium saucepan. Bring to a boil over medium heat. Reduce heat to low; cover and simmer 20 minutes, stirring occasionally.

2. Meanwhile, cook shells according to package directions, omitting salt. Rinse under cold water; drain. Preheat oven to 350°F. Spread thin layer of sauce in bottom of 11×8-inch baking pan.

3. Crumble tofu in medium bowl. Stir in green onions, Parmesan cheese, parsley, basil, salt and pepper. Stuff shells with tofu mixture (about 1 heaping tablespoon per shell). Place shells, stuffed side up, in single layer in prepared pan. Pour remaining sauce evenly over shells.

4. Cover tightly with foil; bake 30 minutes. Remove foil; sprinkle with mozzarella cheese. Bake, uncovered, 5 to 10 minutes or until hot and bubbly.

Makes 4 servings

HOT AND SPICY SPUDS

4 medium baking potatoes

1 cup chopped onion

½ cup chopped green bell pepper

2 cloves garlic, minced

1 teaspoon olive oil

1 can (about 15 ounces) reduced-sodium kidney beans,
   rinsed and drained

1 can (about 14 ounces) no-salt-added tomatoes,
   cut up and undrained

1 can (4 ounces) diced mild green chiles

¼ cup chopped fresh cilantro or parsley

1 teaspoon ground cumin

1 teaspoon chili powder

¼ teaspoon ground red pepper

¼ cup reduced-fat sour cream

¼ cup (1 ounce) shredded reduced-fat Cheddar cheese

1. Preheat oven to 350°F. Scrub potatoes; pierce with fork. Bake 1¼ to 1½ hours or until tender.

2. Meanwhile, spray 2-quart saucepan with nonstick cooking spray; heat saucepan over medium heat. Cook and stir onion, bell pepper and garlic in oil until vegetables are tender. Stir in beans, tomatoes, chiles, cilantro, cumin, chili powder and red pepper. Bring to a boil over high heat. Reduce heat to medium-low. Cover; simmer 8 minutes, stirring occasionally.

3. Gently roll potatoes to loosen pulp. Cut crisscross slit in each potato. Place potatoes on four plates. Press potato ends to open slits. Spoon bean mixture over potatoes. Top with sour cream and sprinkle with cheese.

Makes 4 servings

POLENTA LASAGNA

4¼ **cups water, divided**

1½ **cups yellow cornmeal**

4 **teaspoons finely chopped fresh marjoram**

2 **medium red bell peppers, chopped**

1 **teaspoon olive oil**

1 **pound fresh mushrooms, sliced**

1 **cup chopped leeks**

1 **clove garlic, minced**

½ **cup (2 ounces) shredded part-skim mozzarella cheese**

2 **tablespoons chopped fresh basil**

1 **tablespoon chopped fresh oregano**

⅛ **teaspoon black pepper**

4 **tablespoons freshly grated Parmesan cheese, divided**

1. Bring 4 cups water to a boil in medium saucepan over high heat. Slowly add cornmeal, stirring constantly. Reduce heat to low; stir in marjoram. Simmer 15 to 20 minutes or until polenta thickens and pulls away from side of pan. Spread in ungreased 13×9-inch baking pan. Cover and chill about 1 hour or until firm.

2. Preheat oven to 350°F. Spray 11×7-inch baking dish with nonstick cooking spray. Place bell peppers and remaining ¼ cup water in food processor or blender; process until smooth.

3. Heat oil in medium nonstick skillet over medium heat. Add mushrooms, leeks and garlic; cook and stir 5 minutes or until leeks are crisp-tender. Stir in mozzarella cheese, basil, oregano and black pepper.

4. Cut cold polenta into 12 (3½-inch) squares; arrange six squares in bottom of prepared dish. Spread with half of bell pepper mixture, half of vegetable mixture and 2 tablespoons Parmesan cheese. Top with remaining six squares of polenta, remaining bell pepper and vegetable mixtures and Parmesan cheese. Bake 20 minutes or until cheese is melted and polenta is golden brown.

Makes 6 servings

CLASSIC FAVORITES

Lean Mean Cheeseburger

LEAN MEAN CHEESEBURGER

1 pound ground beef (95% lean)

2 tablespoons quick-cooking oats

½ teaspoon steak seasoning blend

4 seeded *or* whole wheat hamburger buns, split

4 slices lowfat cheese, such as Cheddar *or* American

TOPPINGS:

Lettuce leaves, tomato slices (optional)

1. Place oats in foodsafe plastic bag. Seal bag securely, squeezing out excess air. Roll over bag with rolling pin to crush oats to a fine consistency.

2. Combine ground beef, oats and steak seasoning blend in large bowl, mixing lightly but thoroughly. Lightly shape into four ½-inch patties.

3. Place patties on grid over medium, ash-covered coals. Grill, covered, 11 to 13 minutes (over medium heat on preheated gas grill, covered, 7 to 8 minutes) until instant-read thermometer inserted horizontally into center registers 160°F, turning occasionally.

4. Line bottom of each bun with lettuce and tomato, if desired; top with burger and cheese slice. Close sandwiches.

Makes 4 servings

COOK'S TIP: Cooking times are for fresh or thoroughly thawed ground beef. Color is not a reliable indicator of ground beef doneness.

recipe courtesy of The Beef Checkoff.

OVEN-BAKED CHICKEN PARMESAN

4 boneless, skinless chicken breast halves (about 1¼ pounds)

1 egg, lightly beaten

¾ cup Italian seasoned dry bread crumbs

1 jar (1 pound 8 ounces) RAGÚ® Old World Style® Pasta Sauce

1 cup shredded mozzarella cheese (about 4 ounces)

1. Preheat oven to 400°F. Dip chicken in egg, then bread crumbs, coating well.

2. In 13×9-inch glass baking dish, arrange chicken. Bake uncovered 20 minutes.

3. Pour Pasta Sauce over chicken, then top with cheese. Bake an additional 10 minutes or until chicken is thoroughly cooked. Serve, if desired, with hot cooked pasta.

Makes 4 servings

CLASSIC FAVORITES

CAVATAPPI WITH SAUSAGE MEATBALLS

8 ounces uncooked cavatappi or rigatoni pasta

½ pound bulk mild Italian sausage

½ pound ground beef

1 onion, chopped

1 can (about 14 ounces) diced tomatoes

1 can (6 ounces) tomato paste

½ teaspoon dried oregano

¼ teaspoon salt

⅓ cup grated Parmesan cheese

1. Cook pasta according to package directions. Drain; set aside.

2. Form sausage into small marble-size meatballs. Brown meatballs in large skillet over medium-high heat 3 minutes, stirring frequently. Remove from skillet. Add beef and onion to same skillet; cook until no longer pink, stirring to break up meat. Drain fat.

3. Stir in meatballs, tomatoes, tomato paste, oregano and salt. Simmer 10 minutes. Stir in pasta. Sprinkle with cheese.

Makes 4 servings

MEAT LOAF CUPCAKES

3 medium potatoes, peeled and chopped

1½ pounds 90% lean ground beef

½ cup finely chopped onion

⅓ cup old-fashioned oats

1 egg

2 tablespoons chopped fresh rosemary

½ cup milk

2 tablespoons butter

1 teaspoon salt

Black pepper

¼ cup snipped fresh chives

1. Preheat oven to 350°F. Place potatoes in medium saucepan; cover with water. Bring to a boil; cook 25 to 30 minutes or until potatoes are fork-tender.

2. Meanwhile, combine beef, onion, oats, egg and rosemary in large bowl; mix well. Divide mixture among 10 standard (2½-inch) muffin cups or silicone liners. Bake 25 minutes or until cooked through (160°F).

3. Beat potatoes, milk, butter, salt and pepper in large bowl with electric mixer at medium speed 3 minutes or until smooth. Place mashed potato mixture in large piping bag fitted with large star tip.

4. Remove meat loaf cupcakes to serving platter. Pipe mashed potatoes on top. Sprinkle with chives.

Makes 10 servings

SPICY BEEF TACOS

- **1 pound boneless beef chuck, cut into 1-inch cubes**
- **Vegetable oil**
- **1 to 2 teaspoons chili powder**
- **1 clove garlic, minced**
- **½ teaspoon salt**
- **½ teaspoon ground cumin**
- **1 can (about 14 ounces) diced tomatoes**
- **12 (6-inch) corn tortillas***
- **1 cup (4 ounces) shredded mild Cheddar cheese**
- **2 to 3 cups shredded iceberg lettuce**
- **1 large fresh tomato, seeded and chopped**
- **Chopped fresh cilantro (optional)**

Or, substitute packaged taco shells for the corn tortillas. Omit steps 4 and 5. Warm taco shells according to package directions.

1. Brown beef in 2 tablespoons hot oil in large skillet over medium-high heat 10 to 12 minutes, turning frequently. Reduce heat to low. Stir in chili powder, garlic, salt and cumin. Cook and stir 30 seconds.

2. Add diced tomatoes with juice. Bring to a boil over high heat. Reduce heat to low. Cover and simmer 1½ to 2 hours until beef is very tender.

3. Using two forks, pull beef into coarse shreds in skillet. Increase heat to medium. Cook, uncovered, 10 to 15 minutes until most of liquid has evaporated. Keep warm.

4. Heat 4 to 5 inches of oil in deep fat fryer or deep saucepan over medium-high heat to 375°F; adjust heat to maintain temperature.

5. For taco shells, place 1 tortilla in taco fryer basket;** close gently. Fry tortilla ½ to 1 minute until crisp and golden. Open basket; gently remove taco shell. Drain on paper towels. Repeat with remaining tortillas.

6. Layer beef, cheese, lettuce and chopped tomato in each taco shell. Garnish with cilantro, if desired.

**Taco fryer baskets are available in large supermarkets and in housewares stores.*

Makes 6 servings

ONION-WINE POT ROAST

- **2 tablespoons olive oil, divided**
- **1 teaspoon salt, divided**
- **½ teaspoon black pepper**
- **1 boneless beef chuck roast (about 3 pounds), trimmed**
- **2 pounds yellow onions, cut in half and thinly sliced**
- **2 tablespoons water**
- **2 cups dry red wine, such as cabernet sauvignon or merlot**

1. Heat 1 tablespoon oil in ovenproof Dutch oven over medium-high heat. Sprinkle ½ teaspoon salt and pepper over beef; place in Dutch oven. Brown beef on both sides. Remove to plate.

2. Add remaining 1 tablespoon oil, onions and remaining ½ teaspoon salt to Dutch oven; cook over medium-high heat 10 minutes, stirring frequently. Stir in water, scraping up any browned bits from bottom of Dutch oven. Reduce heat to medium; partially cover and cook 15 minutes or until onions are deep golden brown, stirring occasionally.

3. Preheat oven to 300°F. Stir in wine. Return beef to Dutch oven with any juices accumulated on plate. Cover and bake 3 hours or until beef is fork-tender.

4. Remove beef from Dutch oven; keep warm. Skim fat from juices; serve with beef.

Makes 6 servings

SERVING SUGGESTION: Serve pot roast over mashed potatoes or hot cooked orzo pasta.

TERIYAKI MEAT LOAF

1 tablespoon vegetable oil

1 package (8 ounces) thinly sliced mushrooms

½ cup chopped green onions

1 package (3 ounces) ramen noodles, any flavor, crushed*

½ cup teriyaki sauce

1 egg, lightly beaten

1½ pounds (24 ounces) ground beef

*Discard seasoning packet.

1. Preheat oven to 375°F.

2. Heat oil in medium skillet over medium-high heat. Add mushrooms; cook and stir 10 minutes. Add green onions; cook and stir 1 minute. Transfer to large bowl. Add noodles, teriyaki sauce and egg; stir well. Fold in beef.

3. Press beef mixture into 8×4-inch loaf pan. Bake 35 to 40 minutes or until cooked through (160°F). Let stand 10 minutes before slicing.

Makes 4 to 6 servings

TIP: Serve leftovers on toasted bread or rolls as a meat loaf sandwich. Also, a great brown bag lunch idea!

SWEET & CRISPY OVEN-BAKED CHICKEN

1 **pound boneless skinless chicken breast halves**

¼ **cup FRENCH'S® Honey Mustard**

1⅓ **cups crushed FRENCH'S® French Fried Onions**

1. Coat chicken with mustard. Dip into French Fried Onions. Place into lightly greased baking pan.

2. Bake at 400°F for 20 minutes or until no longer pink in center.

Makes 4 servings

FISH & CHIPS

¾ **cup all-purpose flour**

½ **cup flat beer *or* lemon-lime carbonated beverage**

  Vegetable oil

4 **medium russet potatoes, each cut into 8 wedges**

  Salt

1 **egg, separated**

1 **pound cod fillets (about 6 to 8 small fillets)**

  Malt vinegar and lemon wedges (optional)

1. Combine flour, beer and 2 teaspoons oil in small bowl. Cover and refrigerate 1 to 2 hours.

2. Pour 2 inches oil into large heavy skillet; heat to 365°F over medium heat. Add potato wedges in batches. (*Do not crowd.*) Fry 4 to 6 minutes or until browned, turning once. (Allow temperature of oil to return to 365°F between batches.) Drain on paper towels; sprinkle lightly with salt. Reserve oil to fry cod.

3. Stir egg yolk into flour mixture. Beat egg white in medium bowl with electric mixer at medium-high speed until soft peaks form. Fold egg white into flour mixture.

4. Return oil to 365°F. Dip fish pieces into batter in batches; fry 4 to 6 minutes or until batter is crispy and brown and fish begins to flake when tested with fork, turning once. (Allow temperature of oil to return to 365°F between batches.) Drain on paper towels. Serve immediately with potato wedges. Sprinkle with vinegar and serve with lemon wedges, if desired.

Makes 4 servings

CLASSIC FAVORITES

SPAGHETTI & MEATBALLS

Nonstick cooking spray

6 **ounces uncooked multigrain or whole wheat spaghetti**

¾ **pound extra-lean ground beef**

¼ **pound hot turkey Italian sausage, casing removed**

1 **egg white**

2 **tablespoons plain dry bread crumbs**

1 **teaspoon dried oregano**

2 **cups tomato-basil pasta sauce**

3 **tablespoons chopped fresh basil**

2 **tablespoons grated Parmesan cheese**

1. Preheat oven to 450°F. Coat baking sheet with nonstick cooking spray. Cook spaghetti according to package directions, omitting salt and fat. Drain; keep warm.

2. Combine beef, sausage, egg white, bread crumbs and oregano in medium bowl; mix well. Shape mixture into 16 (1½-inch) meatballs. Place on prepared baking sheet; coat with cooking spray. Bake 12 minutes, turning once.

3. Pour pasta sauce into large skillet; add meatballs. Cook and stir over medium heat 9 minutes or until sauce is heated through and meatballs are cooked through (160°F). Divide spaghetti among four plates. Top with meatballs and sauce; sprinkle with basil and Parmesan cheese.

Makes 4 servings

OVEN-FRIED CHICKEN

6 **boneless skinless chicken thighs (about 1 pound)**

½ **cup milk**

½ **cup all-purpose flour**

1½ **cups crushed cornflakes**

½ **teaspoon salt**

¼ **teaspoon garlic powder**

½ **teaspoon paprika**

¼ **teaspoon black pepper**

2 **tablespoons butter, melted**

1. Place chicken in medium bowl. Add milk; refrigerate 1 hour.

2. Preheat oven to 350°F. Spray baking sheet with slight rim with nonstick cooking spray. Place flour in shallow dish. Combine cornflakes, salt, garlic powder, paprika and pepper in separate shallow dish.

3. Drain chicken; discard milk. Pat chicken dry. Lightly dust chicken with flour. Brush with melted butter. Press chicken into cornflake mixture, generously coating both sides. Arrange on prepared baking sheet.

4. Bake 35 to 40 minutes or until cooked through, turning chicken over after 20 minutes.

Makes 6 servings

RAGÚ® PIZZA BURGERS

1 pound ground beef

2 cups RAGÚ® Old World Style® Pasta Sauce, divided

1 cup shredded mozzarella cheese (about 4 ounces), divided

¼ teaspoon salt

6 English muffins, split and toasted

1. In small bowl, combine ground beef, ½ cup Pasta Sauce, ½ cup cheese and salt. Shape into 6 patties. Grill or broil until done.

2. Meanwhile, heat remaining pasta sauce. To serve, arrange burgers on muffin halves. Top with remaining cheese, sauce and muffin halves.

Makes 6 servings

CHEESY TACO MEATLOAF

2 pounds ground beef

1 jar (16 ounces) PACE® Picante Sauce

1 cup crushed tortilla chips

½ cup shredded Cheddar cheese

1. Thoroughly mix the beef, **⅔ cup** picante sauce and tortilla chips in a large bowl. Place the beef mixture into a 3-quart shallow baking pan and shape into an 8×4-inch loaf.

2. Bake at 350°F. for 1 hour or until the meatloaf is cooked through.

3. Sprinkle the meatloaf with the cheese. Bake for 5 minutes or until the cheese is melted. Heat the remaining picante sauce in a 1-quart saucepan over medium heat to a boil. Serve the sauce with the meatloaf.

Makes 8 servings

CLASSIC FAVORITES

ACKNOWLEDGMENTS

The publisher would like to thank the companies and organizations listed below for the use of their recipes and photos in this publication.

Campbell Soup Company

Del Monte Foods

Ortega®, A Division of B&G Foods North America, Inc.

Reckitt Benckiser, LLC.

Sargento® Foods, Inc.

The Beef Checkoff

Unilever

METRIC CONVERSION CHART

VOLUME MEASUREMENTS (dry)

1/8 teaspoon = 0.5 mL
1/4 teaspoon = 1 mL
1/2 teaspoon = 2 mL
3/4 teaspoon = 4 mL
1 teaspoon = 5 mL
1 tablespoon = 15 mL
2 tablespoons = 30 mL
1/4 cup = 60 mL
1/3 cup = 75 mL
1/2 cup = 125 mL
2/3 cup = 150 mL
3/4 cup = 175 mL
1 cup = 250 mL
2 cups = 1 pint = 500 mL
3 cups = 750 mL
4 cups = 1 quart = 1 L

VOLUME MEASUREMENTS (fluid)

1 fluid ounce (2 tablespoons) = 30 mL
4 fluid ounces (1/2 cup) = 125 mL
8 fluid ounces (1 cup) = 250 mL
12 fluid ounces (1 1/2 cups) = 375 mL
16 fluid ounces (2 cups) = 500 mL

WEIGHTS (mass)

1/2 ounce = 15 g
1 ounce = 30 g
3 ounces = 90 g
4 ounces = 120 g
8 ounces = 225 g
10 ounces = 285 g
12 ounces = 360 g
16 ounces = 1 pound = 450 g

DIMENSIONS

1/16 inch = 2 mm
1/8 inch = 3 mm
1/4 inch = 6 mm
1/2 inch = 1.5 cm
3/4 inch = 2 cm
1 inch = 2.5 cm

OVEN TEMPERATURES

250°F = 120°C
275°F = 140°C
300°F = 150°C
325°F = 160°C
350°F = 180°C
375°F = 190°C
400°F = 200°C
425°F = 220°C
450°F = 230°C

BAKING PAN SIZES

Utensil	Size in Inches/Quarts	Metric Volume	Size in Centimeters
Baking or	8×8×2	2 L	20×20×5
Cake Pan	9×9×2	2.5 L	23×23×5
(square or	12×8×2	3 L	30×20×5
rectangular)	13×9×2	3.5 L	33×23×5
Loaf Pan	8×4×3	1.5 L	20×10×7
	9×5×3	2 L	23×13×7
Round Layer	8×1½	1.2 L	20×4
Cake Pan	9×1½	1.5 L	23×4
Pie Plate	8×1¼	750 mL	20×3
	9×1¼	1 L	23×3
Baking Dish	1 quart	1 L	—
or Casserole	1½ quart	1.5 L	—
	2 quart	2 L	—